THE 30-SECOND GUIDE TO
COACHING *your* INNER CRITIC

D1517516

Susan Mackenty Brady

ISBN: 978-0-9909623-0-4 (sc)
ISBN: 978-0-9909623-1-1 (e)

Lulu Publishing Services rev. date: 12/09/2014

Linkage
Developing Leaders Worldwide

INTRODUCTION

Do you ever hear a critical voice in your head that whispers *"He is an idiot!"*?
Do you ever hear a critical voice in your head that whispers *"I am an idiot!"*?

If you are like most people, you forge ahead, rarely giving thought to how these messages might be impacting your life. But they do...

I offer this guide to you as a fellow journeyer—one who is working hard (and laughing a lot) about how creative the **inner critic** can get, and how skillful the **inner coach** needs to be!

Susan Mackenty Brady
2014

WHAT IS THE
Our inner
in our hea
Critical of others
and
THEY ARE STUPID.
HE JUST DOESN'T GET IT.

NNER CRITIC?

tic is the voice
hat plays

I CAN'T BELIEVE
I SAID THAT.

I AM STUPID.

Critical of self

THE CRITIC?

... our belief
that we are
less than others
or
not enough

IF
ONLY
I
WAS
GOOD
ENOUGH.

WHAT DOES THE

- risk of alienation
- PEOPLE BECOME GUARDED
- loss of engagement, trust, honesty
- loss of loyalty in relationships
- LIMITS ABILITY TO LEARN

Believing we are better than others feels good to us and diminishes others.

- skews ability to make sound decisions

- BECOMING UNAPPROACHABLE
- Affects Our Perception Of Others' Perceptions Of Us

RITIC COST US?

- MISSED OPPORTUNITY
- Underachieving
  - headaches
- Loss of sleep
- gray hair
- guilt
  - POOR SELF-IMAGE

Believing we are not as good as others diminishes us and makes us feel bad about ourselves.

- depression
- OVER-EATING
- Not Living up to Potential
- NOT TAKING CARE OF OURSELVES
- negative impacts on relationships
- downward spiral

BECOME YOUR OWN INNER CRITIC COACH

WHAT DOES TH

What if we
Right Sized
our self-image
and treated ourselves & others
with **Kindness**
and **Respect?**

COACH

a life with

Your inner coach is your internal observer, th
saying, feeling, and why?" This internal observ

COACH OFFER?

We are all imperfect beings. Treating ourselves & others with respect doesn't mean we ask less from ourselves or others. It means we are **Less harsh, More gentle** as we do the asking.

out harshness

oice that asks "What am I thinking, doing, llows you to notice and then change.

WHY COACH TH

We move between being critical of ourselves and being critical of others
all day.
Every day.

INNER CRITIC?

This is **exhausting**.
And it causes us and those around us
unnecessary pain.

Right sizing our self-image
is a choice. An awareness.
A way of thinking.
A moment-by-moment practice.
What it takes is self-awareness and willingness
to change...

HOW TO COACH

PAUSE.

Right size our self-image from "better than others" —thinking we get it and others don't— to getting respectfully curious.

> NO ONE IS PERFECT.
> NOT ME. NOT THEM.
> WHAT MIGHT THEY SEE, KNOW, OR HAVE TO OFFER?

THE

R

NO BETTER OR

THE INNER CRITIC

Right size our self-image from "less than others" —thinking we are not good enough— to holding ourselves in warm regard.

I AM ENOUGH.

STINATION IS

SPECT:

S THAN ANYBODY ELSE.

4 Tips

for
coaching
your
inner
critic

① PUSH THE PAUSE BUTTON

Stimuli will come your way and you will want to react.

Mentally push pause. This will give you **time** to:

◎ TAKE A BREATH.

◎ Right size YOUR SELF-IMAGE

◎ MAKE A CONSCIOUS CHOICE ABOUT YOUR REACTION.

2 BE GENTLE WITH YOURSELF

Pushing pause is hard, especially when we think we are right or when we are flooded with emotion. Like any other practice, we won't get it right every time. **Doing this imperfectly is better than not doing it at all.**

3 RIGHT SIZE BEFORE YOU SPEAK

If we speak while our inner critic has the microphone we risk acting superior or inferior.

People have a hard enough time hearing us, without us sounding "better than" or "less than" others.
Right size your self-image: then speak.

4 PRACTICE GENUINE CURIOSITY

Ask Yourself:

◎ "What might I learn from this person or situation?"

◎ "How do they add value or offer a different view that can help or enrich a situation?"

The only hope we have for being genuinely curious is believing that we have something to learn from others.

In order to believe this we must right size first.

Time to Practice: Notice your Inner Critic and write down what you're hearing... You may notice some themes!

Time to Practice: Notice your Inner Critic and write down what you're hearing... You may notice some themes!

Time to Practice: Notice your Inner Critic and write down what you're hearing... You may notice some themes!

Time to Practice: Notice your Inner Critic and write down what you're hearing... You may notice some themes!

ABOUT US

Susan Brady is an expert in the Inner Critic ☺, an Executive Vice President and Lead Strategist for Linkage's Advancing Women & Inclusion Practice, and an Executive Coach & speaker. She is co-founder and chair of the Women in Leadership Institute™ and lives in the Boston area with her husband and two daughters.

Aftab Erfan is a visual facilitator based in Vancouver, Canada. Her business, Whole Picture Thinking, helps groups see situations more vividly and fully through visuals. She works in the areas of organizational storytelling, strategic thinking, conflict engagement & leadership development. She reluctantly shares her colored pencils with her partner and two sons.

≈ We would like to acknowledge our enthusiastic supporters and gentle critics who have made this project possible. You are too many to name, but you know who you are. Thank you. ≈

Linkage is a global leadership consulting and training firm that works with leaders and leadership teams worldwide to build organizations that produce superior results.